Canada's Governing Bodies
The Crown

Simon Rose

Weigl

Published by Weigl Educational Publishers Limited
6325 10th Street SE
Calgary, Alberta T2H 2Z9
Website: www.weigl.ca

Library and Archives Canada Cataloguing in Publication

Rose, Simon, 1961-, author
      The Crown / Simon Rose.

(Canada's governing bodies)
Issued in print and electronic formats.
ISBN 978-1-4872-0009-1 (bound).--ISBN 978-1-4872-0010-7 (pbk.).--
ISBN 978-1-4872-0011-4 (ebook)

      1. Monarchy--Canada--Juvenile literature. 2. Heads of state--
Canada--Juvenile literature. I. Title.

JL88.R68 2014   j320.471   C2014-901452-X
                                                 C2014-901453-8

Printed in the United States of America in North Mankato, Minnesota
1 2 3 4 5 6 7 8 9 0 18 17 16 15 14

062014
WEP110614

Project Coordinator: Aaron Carr
Editor: Frances Purslow
Art Director: Terry Paulhus

Photo Credits:
Getty: page 6, page 6 top, page 8, page 10 top, page 11 top, page 11 bottom,
page 12 top, page 17 top, page 17 middle, page 17 bottom left, page 17 bottom
right, page 20 top, page 20, page 22, page 23, page 24 top, page 24 bottom, page
25 top, page 25 middle, page 25 bottom, page 26 top, page 26, page 27, page 28
Alamy: page 1, page 4, page 10, page 15
Newscom: page 7, page 8 top, page 9, page 12, page 14 left, page 14 middle,
page 14 right, page 15 left, page 15 middle, page 15 right, page 18, page 19
iStockphoto: page 3

Every reasonable effort has been made to trace ownership and to obtain
permission to reprint copyright material. The publishers would be pleased
to have any errors or omissions brought to their attention so that they may
be corrected in subsequent printings.

We acknowledge the financial support of the Government of Canada through
the Canada Book Fund for our publishing activities.

Contents

Canada's Government

Canada is run by a type of government called representative **democracy**. This means that Canadians vote to elect the politicians who will represent them in government. These elected officials make decisions that affect the daily lives of all Canadians.

Canada's principles of government are based on those of Great Britain. British ideas about politics first came to Canada when Canada was a **colony** of Great Britain. When Canada later became a country, these ideas formed the basis of the government. However, they were changed to suit Canada's unique circumstances.

Canada has different levels of government. Each level has different powers and duties. The **federal** government manages issues that concern all Canadians. Provincial and territorial governments look after the needs of the provinces and territories. Municipal governments make **by-laws** for cities and towns. Some of Canada's Aboriginal Peoples also have their own governments, called band councils. Band councils make decisions that affect people living on **reserves**.

Thomas Mackay, a lumber baron, built Rideau Hall in 1838. It did not become the residence of the governor general until 1867.

Canada has two houses of **parliament**. They are called the House of Commons and the Senate. The House of Commons is also called the lower house. The Senate is called the upper house.

The main centre of Canada's government is Parliament Hill in Ottawa. This is Canada's capital city. The House of Commons and the Senate are located in the Parliament Buildings.

The Centre Block of the Parliament Buildings contains the Peace Tower. This tower stands for Canada's commitment to peace around the world.

The Federal System

Canada's Federal Government

* Creates laws for the whole country
* Has clearly defined powers and areas of responsibility
* Works closely with other levels of government
* Helps to protect the interests of all Canadians

The Parliament of Canada is made up of three parts. These are the House of Commons, the Senate, and the monarch. Each part has a distinct role. The two main decision-making bodies of the federal government are the House of Commons and the Senate. Only they can make laws.

The monarch gives final approval for a **bill** to become law. This is called Royal Assent. The current monarch is Queen Elizabeth II. She is the queen of England and also the queen of Canada. However, the role of the monarch in Canada is mostly **symbolic**. In the Canadian government, the monarch is called the Crown. The Crown rarely turns down any bill that has been passed by the House of Commons and the Senate. The governor general represents the queen in Canada and gives final approval to government **legislation**.

Canada's Senate has a throne for the monarch. When the monarch is not present, the governor general sits in the monarch's place.

Some of the federal government's duties include national defence, banking and currency, **taxation**, and criminal law. The federal government is also responsible for foreign affairs and for deciding who can move to Canada and become Canadian citizens. Sometimes the federal, provincial, and territorial governments work together to make decisions.

Another vital part of the federal government is the Supreme Court. It is the most important legal body in Canada. Judges in the Supreme Court make key decisions that affect the whole country.

Organization of the Canadian Government

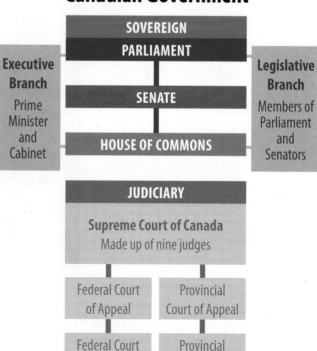

	SOVEREIGN	
Executive Branch Prime Minister and Cabinet	**PARLIAMENT**	**Legislative Branch** Members of Parliament and Senators
	SENATE	
	HOUSE OF COMMONS	

JUDICIARY

Supreme Court of Canada
Made up of nine judges

Federal Court of Appeal	Provincial Court of Appeal
Federal Court of Canada	Provincial Courts

The Crown

In Canada

* Queen Elizabeth II of Great Britain is the head of state
* The governor general carries out the queen's official duties
* The Crown has little power and is mostly symbolic

Canada is a democracy. It is an **independent** country with an elected government in the House of Commons. The prime minister is the head of the government. However, the country is also a monarchy. The current monarch of Great Britain, Elizabeth II, is also the queen of Canada. She is Canada's official **head of state**. The queen rarely visits Canada in person. Instead, the governor general carries out her duties.

The governor general has no real power, but still plays a key role in Canadian government.

A lieutenant governor serves as the monarch's representative in each province. In 1799, Sir Robert Shore Milnes was named the lieutenant governor of Lower Canada, which included parts of modern day Quebec and Labrador.

The governor general opens and closes Parliament. No bill becomes law until the governor general grants Royal Assent. Prime ministers, **cabinet** ministers, judges, and senators are appointed by the Crown. However, the governor general typically approves everything presented by the prime minister.

The Crown is also part of each provincial government. A lieutenant governor represents the monarch in official ceremonies and events in each of Canada's provinces. He or she also has official duties with the provincial **legislatures**. These are similar to the governor general's duties at the federal level. In Canada's territories, this role is filled by commissioners.

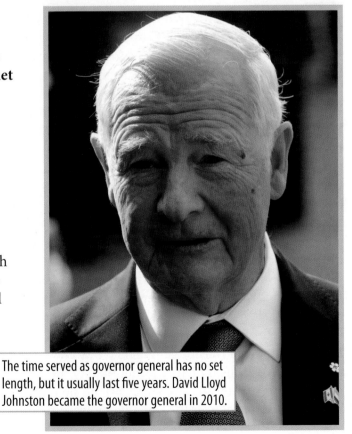

The time served as governor general has no set length, but it usually last five years. David Lloyd Johnston became the governor general in 2010.

History of the Crown

The Crown Originally

* Represented the British government
* Acted as an advisor to the prime minister
* Was a British citizen

T he role of the Crown in Canada is based in Canada's history as a British colony. Before **Confederation** in 1867, Canada was ruled directly by the British. However, the monarch could not be in Canada in person. Local governors acted in Canada for them.

When the Dominion of Canada was created in 1867, Charles Stanley Monck, 4th Viscount Monck, became the first governor general. He was a representative of the British government in Canada's political system. The early governors general advised Canadian prime ministers, but they mostly stayed behind the scenes. The position soon became **ceremonial**. Canada's elected government had the real power. The governor general did not usually interfere in Canadian politics, even though he was allowed to at that time. In 1926, Sir Julian Byng was the governor general. He and Prime Minister Mackenzie King had a disagreement that later led to the role of the governor general being changed. By the 1930s, the governor general had become a representative of the monarch rather than of the British government. This meant that Great Britain no longer had any real control over the Canadian government.

Sir Julian Byng was the commander of the Canadian Corps during the Battle of Vimy Ridge.

After World War II, Canada became more independent of Britain. In 1952, Prime Minister Louis St. Laurent appointed the first Canadian-born governor general. His name was Vincent Massey. It was decided that English and French Canadians would alternate as governor general.

Though the Crown now has little real power, the governor general still has many official duties as Canada's head of state and as the representative of the monarchy. The governor general represents Canada when visiting other countries. He or she also visits Canadian troops. The governor general manages the Canadian Honours System, presenting medals and awards to Canadians for outstanding service.

Vincent Massey was president of the Arts and Letters' Club in Toronto in 1920.

Charles Stanley Monck, 4th Viscount Monck, served as governor general from 1867 to 1868.

CHANGES OVER TIME

1931 The Statute of Westminster states that the governor general is a representative of the monarch, not the British government.

1937 Lord Tweedsmuir makes the first **state visit** by a governor general. He visits President Franklin Roosevelt at the White House and addresses the U.S. Senate.

1947 The governor general becomes Canada's commander-in-chief, in charge of the country's armed forces. This position used to be held by the monarch.

Role of the Crown

The Crown

* Grants Royal Assent to legislation
* Makes official appointments
* Opens and closes Parliament
* Gives the speech from the throne

The ceremonial duties of the governor general are a key part of the Canadian government. Most bills are introduced first in the House of Commons. If the bill is passed by the Commons, it is sent to the Senate. If both houses pass the bill, it then must be approved by the monarch before it becomes law. This is known as the Royal Assent and is performed by the governor general.

A general election in Canada determines who becomes prime minister. The governor general invites the leader of the party with the most seats in the Commons to form a government. This is just a formality. As well, the governor general appoints other government officials. However, the prime minister chooses who is appointed.

Michaëlle Jean served as governor general from 2005 to 2010. During that time, she worked to advance human rights and represented Canada around the world.

The governor general announces the official opening and dissolving of Parliament. Again, this is always on the advice of the prime minister. Elections must take place every four years or when the government loses a **vote of confidence** in the Commons. The prime minister then asks the governor general to dissolve Parliament for an election.

The opening of Parliament is a formal ceremony, in which the governor general explains the government's plans for the coming session of Parliament. The governor general makes the speech from the throne in the Senate **chamber**. This is a speech written by the governing party and read by the governor general at the opening of Parliament. It outlines the planned legislation for the next session. Members of the Senate and Commons are in the chamber to hear this speech. The speech is prepared by the prime minister's office.

POWERS OF THE GOVERNOR GENERAL

Although the Crown is symbolic, the governor general does have powers that can be used in an emergency. These include vetoing a law, refusing permission for a government appointment, or even dismissing the prime minster and appointing a new one. However, these powers are rarely, if ever, used.

How a Bill Is Passed

The governor general, representing the Crown, has a role in the creation of laws in Canada. A proposal to make a new law or to change an existing law begins as a bill in Parliament. Each bill is read three times in both the House of Commons and the Senate. There are five steps before a bill can be passed and receive Royal Assent.

1 The 1st Reading

In the House of Commons, a bill is read for the first time and is printed. The bill becomes part of the official record. There is no **debate** or vote at this stage.

2 The 2nd Reading

Members of Parliament (MPs) debate the bill in the House of Commons. They discuss whether the bill will meet the needs of Canadians. Sometimes, they decide that the bill is a good idea, but it may need to be studied in more detail. If a bill passes at second reading, it then goes to the **committee** stage.

3 Committee Stage

Committee members study the content of the bill. They may also hold hearings if they need more information. At the hearings, experts provide more details on the bill. Once the study is done, the committee may ask for changes to the bill. These are known as amendments. The committee then writes a report on their findings. It may recommend accepting the bill, rejecting it, or making amendments.

The prime minister and the cabinet members must swear an oath at Rideau Hall after an election.

4 Report Stage

If changes to the bill are recommended, the report must be debated in the Commons. The amendments are then accepted, amended further, or rejected. If the committee recommends adopting the bill without any changes, there is no report stage. The bill then moves to third reading.

5 The 3rd Reading

The bill is debated again at third reading. Members who voted for the bill at second reading sometimes change their minds. This is because they may think differently about the amendments. After this debate, the House of Commons votes on the bill for the final time. If the bill is passed, it is sent to the Senate. Similar readings, committees, and reports take place in the Senate.

6 Royal Assent

Once both chambers agree on a final version of the bill, it is granted Royal Assent by the governor general. The bill becomes law.

The Governor General's Home

The governor general has two **official residences**, Rideau Hall in Ottawa and La Citadelle in Quebec City. Rideau Hall has been the official residence and workplace of every governor general of Canada since 1867. It is larger than the official residences of the prime minister and the leader of the **opposition**. The main building has about 175 rooms. The residence is open to the public for tours.

1 The Entrance Hall

The entrance hall was completed in 1913. Over the years, portraits, flags, and coats of arms have been added to the area. The front entrance is where foreign leaders, veterans, and members of the public receiving honours are welcomed to Rideau Hall.

② The Tent Room

The Tent Room was built in 1876 as an indoor tennis court. It was also used to host events. At these times, striped canvas was draped over the walls and ceiling, making the room look like the inside of a tent. The room still has striped decor to honour this history. It also has portraits of Queen Victoria and past governors general.

③ The Ballroom

The ballroom of Rideau Hall is used for ceremonies. This is where the prime minister takes the oath of office. The ballroom is also used for entertaining foreign leaders and for presenting awards and medals to Canadian citizens.

④ The Pauline Vanier Room

The Pauline Vanier Room is also known as the Canadian Room. It is used for small meetings and interviews with people receiving a **Governor General's Award**. It is named after the wife of former governor general Georges Vanier, who added Canadian art and furniture to the residence.

⑤ The Reception Room

The Reception Room is the oldest part of Rideau Hall. This room is used to welcome people who will be taking part in a ceremony. They are told what their role will be, so they know what to expect. These events include the taking of oaths of office by cabinet ministers or presentations of the National Aboriginal Achievement Awards.

Key Positions of the Crown

Once in office, the governor general stays in direct contact with the queen. Throughout the year, he or she undertakes many duties on the monarch's behalf. The office of the secretary to the governor general (OSGG) supports the governor general in these duties and activities. The OSGG employs about 190 people.

Secretary to the Governor General

The secretary is the governor general's senior advisor. He or she manages the office at Rideau Hall and at La Citadelle in Quebec City. The secretary manages the Canadian Heraldic Authority (CHA). The CHA creates and grants new coats of arms, flags, and badges to Canadian companies and individuals. The secretary is also the secretary general of the Order of Canada. The Order of Canada is awarded to people who have made the world better by their actions.

Deputy Secretary, Policy, Program and Protocol Branch

The deputy secretary ensures that official events follow the formal rules and procedures for government affairs. He or she also oversees events or services for visitors and keeps the public informed about what the governor general is doing. The deputy secretary manages housekeeping and maintenance staff at Rideau Hall and at La Citadelle.

The Order of Canada was established in 1967.

Deputy Secretary of Honours

The deputy secretary of honours manages the Canadian Honours System, including the CHA. The honours system was created to recognize Canadians who have made important contributions to the country and the world.

Director General, Corporate Services

The director general keeps track of how much money is spent by the governor general's office. He or she manages the workings of the office, including its equipment, supplies, and staff.

 ## HOW ARE THE GOVERNORS GENERAL APPOINTED?

Until 2010, the prime minister chose the governor general, who usually serves for five years. That year, Prime Minister Stephen Harper created a special committee to search for the best candidate to be the next governor general. They selected David Johnston, and the monarch officially approved the choice. The committee has since been made permanent. It is called the Advisory Committee on Vice-Regal Appointments. The committee will also be in charge of searching for suitable candidates for lieutenant governor and commissioner positions.

When selecting likely candidates for governor general, it is traditional to alternate between English and French Canadians. The committee also has to look for someone who has given outstanding service to Canada, who represents all Canadians, and who has no political background or links to any political party.

Once appointed to the position of governor general, a person attends an investiture ceremony to be confirmed. The ceremony for former governor general Adrienne Clarkson was held on October 7, 1999.

A Day in the Life

The Crown

✤ **Is the commander-in-chief of Canadian Armed Forces**

✤ **Honours outstanding Canadians**

✤ **Promotes national identity and unity**

✤ **Hosts foreign officials who visit Canada**

✤ **Acts as an ambassador for Canada**

The governor general undertakes many different roles and duties. One such role is the commander-in-chief of the Canadian Armed Forces. However, he or she does not make military decisions. The governor general appoints military officials based on the advice of the prime minister and the minister of national defence. The governor general also presents military honours.

Other awards presented by the governor general include the Order of Canada and the Caring Canadian Award, given to outstanding caregivers and volunteers. The governor general is also the head of the Canadian Heraldic Authority.

Promoting national identity and unity is another key duty of the governor general. He or she travels across Canada to attend cultural and community events, meeting Canadians in their communities. The governor general also visits schools and hospitals and meets with Canadians at both official residences in Ottawa and Quebec City.

On March 18, 2014, Governor General David Johnston greeted the last Canadian soldiers to return from Afghanistan as they exited their plane in Ottawa.

The governor general welcomes world leaders when they visit Canada. Official receptions take place at Rideau Hall or La Citadelle. The governor general also receives foreign **ambassadors** when they first arrive in Ottawa.

When making state visits to other countries, the governor general serves as Canada's ambassador. On trips abroad, the governor general is joined by **delegates** from different parts of Canada. On these visits, the governor general promotes Canadian values, culture, trade, and commerce.

LETTERS OF CREDENCE

Before they can begin work, new ambassadors from other countries are welcomed to Canada by the governor general. He or she grants the new ambassadors official documents known as Letters of Credence. These documents recognize the ambassadors as their country's representatives. The governor general also signs documents for new Canadian ambassadors before they begin work in another country.

Important Moments

The governor general's role is mainly symbolic. However, the Crown has been involved in many key moments in Canadian history.

The King-Byng Affair 1926

By the 1920s, the monarch no longer held much power in Canada. The governor general was expected to follow the prime minister's advice. In 1924, Liberal Prime Minister Mackenzie King lost the election but could still form a government with the support of another party. In 1926, King asked the governor general, Sir Julian Byng, to dissolve Parliament and call a general election. Byng refused. Instead, he invited the Conservative Party leader to form a new government. This was within his powers, but many people did not agree with his decision. The Conservatives then took over, but only stayed in power a few days. King won a majority in the next election. He asked the British government to change the governor general's role. The governor general could no longer interfere in Canadian politics.

The Statute of Westminster 1931

In 1931, the Statute of Westminster removed the power British Parliament had over Canada. The federal government and the provinces could not agree on rules for changing Canada's **constitution**. This led to the British government maintaining the power to change Canada's constitution for another 50 years. The position of High Commissioner was created and was similar to a British ambassador to Canada. Governors general became representatives of the monarch, not the British government. After 1931, governors general would be appointed by the monarch. However, they would always follow the advice of the Canadian prime minister.

The Constitution Act 1982

In 1982, Canada's new constitution removed the country's final links to Great Britain. The Constitution Act contains many important clauses, including the Canadian Charter of Rights and Freedoms. Although Canada is no longer connected to Great Britain, Queen Elizabeth II is still queen of Canada. The Crown continues to be part of the Canadian system of government. The Act states that the federal government and all the provinces must approve any future changes to the Crown in Canada. This includes the position of governor general.

The Canadian Heraldic Authority 1988

Canadians have always been able to have a **coat of arms**. A coat of arms is usually a unique design painted on a shield. Up until 1988, Canadians who wanted a coat of arms had to apply to England or Scotland. However, on June 4, 1988, this power was given to Canada when the Canadian Heraldic Authority was created.

Prorogation of Parliament 2008

In December 2008, Prime Minister Stephen Harper faced a confidence vote in the Commons. This could have defeated his **minority** Conservative government. He asked governor general Michaëlle Jean to **prorogue**, or suspend, Parliament to help his government. The governor general could have dissolved Parliament and called for an election. She could also have asked Harper to resign, so that the opposition parties could form a government. The governor general decided to suspend Parliament for seven weeks. The Conservatives avoided defeat, but the decision angered many people. Many MPs believed that a government should not use prorogation for its own interests.

Significant Governors General

Many men and women have served as governor general since the Dominion of Canada was first established in 1867. For almost the next 100 years, governors general were usually British noblemen. Most had served in the military. The first Canadian-born governor general was appointed in 1952. The first female governor general was appointed in 1984. Some governors general have played key roles in Canadian society. Others have made important contributions to Canadian history.

Sir Julian Byng – 1921 to 1926

Sir Julian Byng (1862–1935) was also known as Lord Byng. He was the British commander of Canadians troops at the Battle of Vimy Ridge in 1917, during World War I. He was a popular choice when he was appointed as governor general in 1921. However, he is also remembered for the King-Byng Affair in 1926. Byng refused Prime Minister Mackenzie King's request to dissolve Parliament. The affair changed the role of the governor general in the Canadian government.

Vincent Massey – 1952 to 1959

Vincent Massey (1887–1967) was the first Canadian to serve as governor-general of Canada. In 1926, he was the first Canadian official to visit the United States as a representative of the Canadian government. He also became the Canadian High Commissioner in London in 1935. As governor general, Massey was a strong supporter of the arts. He helped to set up the **Canada Council** in 1957. He travelled to many parts of the country during his term. Massey often talked about the country's many different cultures, languages, and traditions. He strongly believed that all Canadians should learn both English and French.

Georges Vanier – 1959 to 1967

Georges Vanier (1888–1967) was Canada's first French-Canadian governor general. Vanier was one of Canada's commanders in World War I. He served with great distinction and lost his right leg during the war. He later served as a diplomat in France and Great Britain. He was appointed governor general in 1959. During his term, Vanier focussed on helping seniors, young people, and the needy. In Quebec, it was also a time of a growing desire to separate from Canada. Vanier worked hard for Canada's national unity.

Jeanne Sauvé – 1984 to 1990

Jeanne Sauvé (1922–1993) was the first woman appointed as governor general. She had formerly been the first female cabinet member from Quebec. She was also the first female Speaker of the House of Commons. As governor general, Sauvé worked hard for peace, national unity, and for young people. She made a number of state visits to Europe, Asia, and South America. Sauvé also travelled within Canada and opened the Winter Olympics in Calgary in 1988. After her retirement, she started the Jeanne Sauvé Youth Foundation.

Adrienne Clarkson – 1999 to 2005

Adrienne Clarkson (born 1939) was the first member of a minority and the first immigrant to become governor general. She was born in Hong Kong and moved to Canada as a **refugee** in 1942. Clarkson grew up in Ottawa. She was a successful journalist and broadcaster before becoming governor general in 1999. As governor general, she travelled across Canada and represented Canada abroad. She also visited Canadian troops stationed overseas in Europe, the Persian Gulf, and Afghanistan.

Issues Facing the Crown

Issues Include

* ❖ *The cost of the governor general*
* ❖ *Canada's ties to the monarchy*
* ❖ *The push toward a Canadian republic*

The cost of supporting the Crown upsets many Canadians who feel that Canada should not keep its ties to the monarchy.

S ome Canadians feel that having a governor general is too expensive. In the mid 2000s, the cost of operating the governor general's office and the offices of all 10 lieutenants governor cost Canadians more than $50 million per year. This includes the cost of running the two official residences and travelling within Canada and to other countries. The governor general also uses services that are paid for by other government departments, such as Foreign Affairs and the Royal Canadian Mounted Police. People feel that this adds up to too much money for what they believe is an unnecessary position.

Some people think the Crown ties Canada to an old-fashioned system. Since the Crown is part of Canada's government, they feel that Canada is not totally independent of Great Britain. Most other countries in the Commonwealth are **republics**. The monarch has no part in their government. If Canada became a republic without a monarch, the country could still be part of the Commonwealth. However, Canada would be a fully independent country and not a monarchy.

However, there are other Canadians who like the country's current system but feel Canada should cut its ties to Great Britain. They think the monarchy should be Canadian and not based on the British royal family. These people argue that it would be better if the monarch was Canadian instead of British. This would better represent Canada's distinct culture and traditions.

Protests over ties to the monarchy extended to a visit from Prince William and Catherine, Duchess of York, during their 2011 visit to Canada.

Know Your Governor General

1 Who was the first Canadian to serve as governor general?

2 Where is the official residence of the governor general?

3 For how long does a governor general usually serve?

4 Who served as the first governor general of Canada?

5 What is Royal Assent?

7 Who prepares the Speech From the Throne that the governor general reads out in the Senate chamber?

6 Who represents the Crown at the provincial level?

8 When was the King-Byng Affair?

9 What is the OSGG?

10 What is La Citadelle?

Further Resources

There are many places online where you can find out more about the Crown, its role in Canada's government system, the work that the governor general does, and the many duties of the office. Websites also cover the history of the monarchy in Canada, key events in Canadian history that involve the Crown, and the men and women who have served as governor general. You can also learn more about issues facing the Crown today.

Learn more about governors general, including their duties and the history of their role in Canada.

❧ www.gg.ca/index.aspx

Discover Rideau Hall, the official residence of Canada's governor general in Ottawa.

❧ www.ncc-ccn.gc.ca/places-to-visit/official-residences/rideau-hall

Learn more about the men and women who have served as governor general of Canada since 1867.

❧ www.gg.ca/document.aspx?id=14615

Join the Debate

What is a debate?

When people debate a topic, two sides take a different viewpoint about one idea. They present logical arguments to support their views. Usually, each person or team is given a set amount of time to present its case. The presenters take turns stating their arguments until the total time set aside for the debate is used up. Sometimes, there is an audience in the room listening to the presentations. Later, the members of the audience vote for the person or team they think made the best arguments.

Debating is an important skill. It helps people to think about ideas carefully. It also helps them develop ways of speaking that others can follow easily. Some schools have debating clubs as part of their after-school activities. Debates are also often held in history classes. Students may debate when they are studying about world events.

The issue below has been debated across Canada. Gather a group of friends or classmates, and divide into teams to debate the issue. Each team should take time to research the issue and develop solid arguments for its side.

? Should the monarchy be abolished?

Some Canadians question whether the monarchy should be retained. Others believe that the Crown is an important part of Canada's heritage.

Yes	No
• The monarchy has no power, is too expensive, and serves no purpose.	• The monarchy makes Canada distinct from the United States and is a symbol of unity.
• An elected official could easily perform the governor general's duties.	• The governor general still has powers that can be used if needed.
• The monarch and his or her family are not interested in Canada and rarely visit the country.	• The monarchy is an important part of Canada's heritage and should be maintained.
• An independent country should not have a foreign monarch.	

Key Words

ambassadors: people who represent their country while visiting another country

bill: legislation presented to Parliament for approval; a bill must be passed by both the House of Commons and the Senate to become law

by-laws: rules passed by municipal governments that are only in effect within the limits of the town or city

cabinet: certain members of Parliament who the prime minister appoints to head government departments and act as advisors

Canada Council: a federal government organization that promotes the arts in Canada

ceremonial: involving little to no authority

chamber: a hall designed for the meetings of a legislative or similar type of assembly

coat of arms: a design usually painted on a shield to represent a person, family, or institution

colony: when a country is ruled by another country and does not have its own government

committee: a group of people with a specific job, such as investigating, discussing, reporting, or acting on an issue

Confederation: the process that created the Dominion of Canada in 1867

constitution: the system of laws and principles that describes the nature, functions, and limits of a government

debate: a discussion in Parliament where different views are presented

delegates: people that a group has chosen to represent them

democracy: a system of government in which leaders are elected by the people

federal: the national government in charge of laws and policies that affect the whole country

Governor General's Award: one of several awards presented to people for achievement in fields such as writing, teaching, and art

head of state: the official holding the highest position in a country; this can be a ceremonial position with little power or an elected president or prime minister

independent: self-governing; not controlled by a outside power

legislation: laws; also the process by which laws are made in a government body

legislatures: provincial governing bodies that make or change laws

minority: people whose race, religion, or culture is different from the main group in a society

official residences: where a country's head of state, prime minister, or president lives

opposition: the political party with the second highest number of seats in the House of Commons after an election

Parliament: the Canadian federal government, including the Crown, the House of Commons, and the Senate

prorogue: to suspend proceedings in Parliament

refugee: a person who flees from his or her country to find a safe place to live

republics: states in which the people and their elected representatives hold the power; an elected or nominated president is head of state

reserves: lands set aside for First Nations by the Canadian government

state visit: a formal visit by a foreign head of state to another country

symbolic: something that is only a symbol and has no real power

taxation: the process by which a government raises money to pay for services

vote of confidence: a vote called to see whether the ruling party should remain in power

Index